C000052378

SHADOW SCRIPT

Published by Newcastle Centre for the Literary Arts,
Newcastle University, 2013

ISBN 978-0-9563837-30

Project curated by Linda Anderson, Director, NCLA

Cover artwork by Kate Sweeney

Typeset by Silbercow

Printed and bound by Field Print, Boldon Colliery

SHADOW SCRIPT

Twelve poems for Lindisfarne and Bamburgh

edited by Colette Bryce

CONTENTS

INTRODUCTION

The monastery on Lindisfarne was founded in the seventh century by St Aidan, an Irish monk from St Columba's monastery on Iona. It is celebrated for the remarkable natural beauty of its setting, for its association with the eighth-century *Lindisfarne Gospels*, and for its famous saint, Cuthbert, to whom the Gospels are partly dedicated. St Columba, or Colm Cille as he is also known, and Iona are thereby linked to Cuthbert of Lindisfarne and to the nearby royal settlement at Bamburgh where St Aidan died, leaning against the church which would later bear his name.

Innovative art, such as that of the *Lindisfarne Gospels*, and the interchange between Irish, Latin, British and English culture, characterizes the 'golden age' of early medieval Northumbrian culture. The book is one of the great early medieval gospel texts, like the equally glorious *Book of Kells* and the *Lichfield* or *Llandeilo Gospels* associated with St Chad, another monk who trained on Lindisfarne.

While there is no evidence that Cuthbert or Aidan were poets (although an early story in the *Life of St Columba* has the saint prophesying the death of a poet!), there is plenty of evidence that each responded powerfully to the poetry of these iconic places of Lindisfarne, the Farne Islands and Iona. Writers such as Bede also took up the challenge; Bede returned to the story of Cuthbert's life on a number of occasions, writing in both metrical poetry and in prose. The earliest accounts of the lives of Cuthbert and Columba (Colm Cille), as well as Aidan, prompt us to consider just how enmeshed their lives were in these island worlds of land and sea.

This pamphlet brings together twelve poets who have strong links with the North East of England and who accepted the challenge to respond to the medieval texts and the haunting landscape with which they are associated, in their own way. The process has involved discussion, reading and two group journeys to Bamburgh and Lindisfarne on a 'poets' bus', one journey undertaken in searing cold and wet, and the other on a brilliant spring day when the vistas stretched for miles, and everything shone.

The poems were written separately, each poet finding their own point of entry into the material, but they also resonate with each other, and should be thought of as a contemporary re-enacting of the multiple voices of medieval texts. Digital artist Tom Schofield has given this even more dramatic form in a sound installation called *Antiphonal*, located in the Lookout Tower on Lindisfarne and the crypt of St Aidan's Church, Bamburgh, during July and August 2013. The voices of the poets are layered digitally, speaking together and in counterpoint with each other, and across the distance separating the different locations. In this pamphlet, the title gestures towards the palimpsestic nature of medieval writing, the often incomplete scraping away of words and re-use of manuscripts for new works. This is given new form in these poems, where images, narratives and words from the past can be seen as shadows in the background, glimmers of meaning, illuminated by their contemporary imagining.

Prof. Linda Anderson, Newcastle University
Prof. Clare Lees, King's College, London

As the tide ebbs and flows, this place is surrounded twice daily by the waves of the sea like an island and twice, when the shore is left dry, it becomes again attached to the mainland.

Bede

Sean O'Brien

LONG WAVE

Whether you stay or go, you hear
The water brushing at the threshold
And the long wave comes and carries you –
Home, home, as far as far,
The compass gathered like a rose
Into its bud, till you are neither
Here nor there, or so you almost know
At dusk and dawn, when time's the only praise
That counts, outsailing its creator.
When the melancholy wave withdraws
Into a patience you can never share,
For half a day and half eternity you wish
To leave yourself marooned and calling
From the shore, until the long wave comes
Climbing past death's stony door again
And spilling over till it seems
Like something you might know, but is a wave,
And not the first word or the last,
Home, home, as far as far,
The compass gathered like a rose.

Colette Bryce

ASYLUM

Iona

Should a guest blow in from the north of Ireland,
   buffeted by the wind,

should the shadow of a cross, afloat on the water,
   mirror the flight of a pilgrim guest

pitching an effortful course through the buffeting gusts,
   this far from the north of Ireland;

should the pilgrim guest, whittled with hunger, depleted
   in reserves, lose altitude

and collapse on the stones of your own small island,
   beaten and worn,

stagger on the shingle, dragging magnificent wings like a cape,
   like an airman trailing his billowing silks,

you must lift this creature and carry it, gathered
   in your arms, over the field to the bothy,

and there, attend to its invalid needs
   for three consecutive days and nights,

during which time it may huddle in a corner, throat retracted
   into its ruff, stern as a cleric, gimlet-eyed,

yet gulping the silver herring you proffer
   like pills, gaining strength, getting well,

till you walk with it back to the narrow beach, on day four,
   watch it take a run

and lift with the gawkiest of take-offs, creaking beats
   of its great span, neck and bill extended like an arrow

pointing the route to my old homeland
   – which is why I am so solicitous of your kindness –

ruling a line straight south to Malin Head
   and home, the sweet district of Ireland.

After Adomnán's account of St Columba's prophecy of the heron

Alistair Elliot

IONA

Near the dead kings, there is a room of stone,
a box of silence.
No sound comes in
from the humming airs of summer.
If you could lift it like a pepperpot
and pierce the trodden floor,
you might season the world of man with quiet.

We aspire
uneasily to the silence of these cells.
There will be plenty of peace when we have gone –
Iona will still be here.
But we have learnt suspicion
elsewhere; it follows us
into this kingdom of the gulls and seals.

For who should we meet, beside the path, but Rex
the African queen
on some queer pilgrimage. We were caught
out of our frames,
and both forgot
ourselves, even our names.
Social confusion hinted guilt and sex,

though nothing was going on. He was alone;
and I, though I was with
somebody else's wife,
was innocent enough:
just crewing for this friendly woman,
the skipper of
that stolen boat there riding in the firth.

As we rowed out to her, aiming across
the tide, strong between islands,
I feared, if we should miss,
we might be carried down and round
to the Garvellachs, where they say
Columba used to hide himself, away
even from the sound
of solitaries and the graves of kings.

Cynthia Fuller

ST CUTHBERT ON INNER FARNE

How the small boat rode the swell
  tossed like flotsam
    steadied by prayer

a cloud of curious fulmars
  circling calling

He left the shared bread
  the community
    of compline

for the kittiwake colony
  the turmoil of terns

choosing solitude among sea birds
  the salt lash of the storm
    inhospitable hermitage

sea cresting and crashing
  sending spray swirling

no silence in the buffeting wind
  but the silence within
    stillness gathered

divine contemplation
  among puffins and eiders

How his spirit grew strong
  icy shallows his abbey
    the night sky his dome

Peter Armstrong

TERNS

He went to the island called Farne, which is in the
midst of the sea and surrounded on every side by
water, a place where, before this, almost no one
could remain alone for any length of time on
account of the various illusions caused by devils.
But he fearlessly put them to flight...

Anonymous Life of Cuthbert

My son was as gentle as the eider
when they drew his blood,
going for the eye, to blind,
or blank all record of the deed.
He says now there's no cloister
without your sweet eye
to give us mind.
Look up and place us here –
heartland, periphery;
the tide's on the flood
and all your homing souls
have quit the scene;
fools, or holy fools,
we're left to the sea's missal,
that cold manual
you might instruct us in.

Did you really drive them out,
hungry as you were
for the empty O of the air?
Or free them
into their blue-white skies,

that bright northerly paradise
to which you'd tune
each coming spring
clear eye and sharp ear
for their return
as a mother might
for her shrill children

Pippa Little

CLOOTY GOSPEL

Winter labour – sacking washed, stretched and sewn
to frame's webbed edge, ready for the hook:
aad claes summer-gathered cut to stripes,
kept spiral-rolled by colour, navy, worsted, black,
once-Sunday-bests of chintzes, slub, forget-me-not:
now we ink in, snarled with supple elements, dot
after dot round saucer's curve, unfurl the track
that, snaking out from curl and twine of leaf, delights
how border, wave, cloud, flow together – look!
unsundered all and whole, the new Farne grown:

slow in furrow the riddled land begins to sprout,
shoots pushed in, hooked out, take chance and bloom
mosses, marram grass, seacoal under weathered hands,
pylon and turbine, windblown tethered mares,
tormentil, northerlies, otters and seals' slicked necks
mewl of cormorants and lambs, our wantings and regrets,
stave, blade, spiral, all of it a readying for prayer –
as a causeway also silvers then grows dull in tidal lands
so Eadfrith's swan-quill pricked out from the gloom
low saffron hillsides, lapis lazuli of high tides slipping out –

you would be happy, Cuthbert, sinking each
poor ulcerated foot deep into these springy tufts, your palms
soothed by cool, tweeded streams, your way
befriended, peopled, made fresh anew
by our labour around the frame, and in the weave
we offer fishing twine, star-grey Cuddy's beads,
(take our turn, our time, knowing we have so few,
only, all of us, our each allotted days)
kiss of indigo on calfskin, shells singing their inward psalm –
use these gifts, Cuthbert, gathered from your beach.

W N Herbert

NORTH OF THE BOOK

1

Cuthbert's cloud crypt is barely blue-flecked.
Beneath it, rapt, his bestial elect
witness the bay as a sunken boat
in which the sea-fowl gospels float.

2

Prior Puffin / arranges fish
upon his profane / palate's dish.

Sister Otter / won't insist
but the bliss of water / is like a kiss.

Brother Crow / can't allow
that a bird might know / how to bow.

Father Gull / holds Bible School
for a fresh lamb's skull / and a crab in a pool.

Mother Whale / dives to foil
the foolish sail / and saves her oil.

Deacon Dolphin / sings descant
to the shoal's cold hymn / in greed's ascent.

Sacristan Seal – / wrack his stained glass –
ecstatic, reels / in the tidal mass.

Hermit Crab / with trembling claws
grabs scuttled garb / and, ragged, withdraws.

Abbess Cod / knows the abyss
is as close to God / as the white cloud is.

Abbot Herring / in a habit of silver
and a crowd of uncaring / is a harp that shivers.

Venerable Bee / levitates
while her harebell history / reverberates.

Saint Snail / can't explain
but his pilgrim trail / is a glittering stain.

3

Northumberland's casket of hills
encloses the holy corruptibles.
North of the book the page is born
from vellum sand and tide's return.

Peter Bennet

AFTER DARK AT LINDISFARNE CASTLE

The great commander of the Gormorants
The Geese and Ganders of these Hallowed lands
                                    Captain Rugg

Here's the upper battery. Here is your ghost.
Thy presence seems composed, dear Captain Rugg,
of moistures of this summer night.
Thou didst not merely command cormorants
but culverins and demi-culverins,
sakers and falconets, master gunners,
a master's mate and then a score of sojers.
At this dainty fort you were a genial host
and strangers did abide. Your bottle nose
became a beacon in the dying light
of Britain's republic. I am not afraid.
Your hauntings hereabouts are just a jest,
thou hoaxer, Sir, thou hock of the hog,
thou gammon! Or are you waiting to be paid
by King or Parliament? You have no wants
your long-due wages could provide for now
methinks. I can make out, by looking through you,
lit windows of *the borowgh towne all sett*
with fishers very poore that is a markett
on ye Satterday, howbeit little used,
and then the tumbling Priory
that is the store-house of the garrison.
Perhaps we might talk poetry?
Like you, your couplets linger on.
But no, your nose swings further east
your finger to your lips and as you fade
I hear from off the Farnes the seals intone
the psalms that Cuthbert taught them as the sun
at dawn walks on the sea. I am alone.

Christy Ducker

ST CUTHBERT BANISHES DEMONS FROM THE LASER CLINIC

He's sad to see my tattoo go
under the laser, blistering
from Lindisfarne knot to hot dough,
I got inked up too young –
too full of hell, I say to him
and he smiles his hermit crab smile,
suggests I think of the Book
his acolyte wrote on skin
with soot and gold, how it reconciles
gannets, cats and dogs as word
of love, how every page is flawed
on purpose, saying to people
perfection makes us much too proud –
wear your mistakes like gospel.

Gillian Allnutt

LINDISFARNE: THE ROUGHS

i

at thorn the wind that sore unshriven thing

ii   **anon**

in truth I was alone

as it had been corrack or coffin

I carried the earth, its poor inscription, on my back

who will remember it

who will remember the sun and the moon

my pillow stones

iii

silent the settlement of stone

iv **cuthbert alone**

hwaet

my whole assent, my heart, my hut

of stone unhewn and turf

and bent

ferann

v

or priory or prayer the wind blows through

vi **in gertrude jekyll's garden**

am drawn, an old reluctance, like the moon

the sea, for example, sings to itself alone its *nunc dimittis*

we are bound to one another, God, my own anon

and of our solitude we are the guardian

vii

perpetual arrival of the sea and of the king acquisitive his people

Linda France

SILVERWEED

Argentina anserina

You send me a pilgrim-monk's-eye view –
our lord's footsteps, cinquefoil – gold and silver
sprung out of the sand, leaves like feathers, spray.
Crimson runners are lines on a manuscript,
join what needs to be joined, arteries

of earth and heart: the shudder of the sea
not far away; a sadness in the stretch
and snap of the waves, the way they suck themselves
back, sadder. You steer your course with such grace,
a brother's footsteps I try to follow,

asking for nothing – amazed when what blooms
in the imprint of each carefully planted heel
and toe is a sudden illumination
of silver and gold, home for the mutual,
that amniotic salt we've been berthed in

over and over. All I need to do
is open the book of my heart and keep on
looking. Here, traveller – *goosewort, richette* –
tuck some fresh leaves inside your shoes
to leaven the crossing, our long walking.

Linda Anderson

AFTERTHOUGHT

After I closed the book there were other openings:
a medley of notes thinning to silence,
phrases of memory, cadences, voices
came back to me. I watched small pockets of light
on the waves, infinite gradations of colour.

Swallows flew casual loops through the air
erasing the meaning of journey, arrival;
the encumbered, lumbering body of a seal
lay on the rocks where Cuthbert waded
and eiders plucked their chests without a thought of him.

The green, unwritten pages of fields stretched away
from the long causeway, from beginnings and endings.
One hare, then another, lolloped through the long grass.
Three deer, beatific, in a field of cabbages,
looked into the distance as if they were saints.

NOTES

PETER ARMSTRONG
*Arctic Tern (Sterna paradisaea)... like most terns, will attack
intruders threatening their nests, often 'dive-bombing' them
with their sharp bills at the ready.* Scottish Wildlife Trust

GILLIAN ALLNUTT
ii A local man, a native of Northumbria, recalls an earlier time
of his life when he was converted from the pagan religion to
Christianity by Aidan and a group of Irish monks who came
from Iona to Lindisfarne in 634.
pillow stones: small stones laid flat on the surface of a grave,
inscribed with a cross and the name of the person buried there.

iv, vii Cuthbert (c635–687) retired in 676 from the monastic
community on Lindisfarne to a hermitage on Farne Island
where he spent nine years in prayer and contemplation. In 685
King Egfrid of Northumbria arrived to ask him to become
Bishop of Lindisfarne. Reluctantly he consented but within two
years returned to his hermitage where he died.
hwaet: an Anglo-Saxon word, an exclamation made at the
beginning of a poem or speech to call for attention.
ferann: 'Farne' comes from *ferann*, a Celtic word meaning 'land'.

vi Gertrude Jekyll: around 1911 she planned the planting of the
old walled garden belonging to the castle on Lindisfarne. It is
still a garden, a sheltered enclosure on the exposed headland, a
safe place in which to sit and listen to the sea.
*Nunc dimitti*s: a prayer from the service of Evensong in the
Anglican Church, named after the opening words of the prayer
in Latin. The words form the Song of Simeon in Luke 2, 29–32.

CONTRIBUTORS

GILLIAN ALLNUTT lives near Durham. Her eighth collection, *indwelling*, is forthcoming from Bloodaxe Books.

LINDA ANDERSON is the author of *Elizabeth Bishop: Lines of Connection* (Edinburgh UP) and a poetry pamphlet *Greenhouse* (Mariscat Press), both published this year. She is Professor of English at Newcastle University and Director of the Newcastle Centre for the Literary Arts.

PETER ARMSTRONG was born in Blaydon upon Tyne and lives in Northumberland. He has published four collections including *The Capital of Nowhere* (Picador) and *The Book of Ogham* (Shoestring, 2012)

PETER BENNET has published six books of poetry. *Border, New and Selected Poems* is forthcoming from Bloodaxe. He lived for over thirty years near the Wild Hills o' Wanney in Northumberland and now lives in Whitley Bay.

COLETTE BRYCE is an Irish poet and editor based in Newcastle. Her three poetry collections are published by Picador and a new one is forthcoming in 2014.

CHRISTY DUCKER lives in Northumberland. Her pamphlet *Armour* (Smith/Doorstop, 2011) was a PBS Choice, and a selection of current work features in *Oxford Poets 2013*.

ALISTAIR ELLIOT has published eight books of his own poems, and has translated works of Heine, Verlaine and Valéry. His version of Euripides' *Medea* reached the West End and Broadway.

LINDA FRANCE's most recent collection is *You are Her* (Arc, 2010). She is the former Leverhulme Poet in Residence at Moorbank Botanic Gardens, and is currently continuing her research into plants and gardens.

CYNTHIA FULLER teaches creative writing at the University of Newcastle upon Tyne. She has published five poetry collections with Flambard Press, most recently *Background Music* in 2009.

W N HERBERT is Professor of Poetry at Newcastle University. His latest collection is *Omnesia* (Bloodaxe, 2013). He lives in a converted lighthouse overlooking the River Tyne at North Shields.

PIPPA LITTLE has lived in Northumberland for over twenty years. Her latest poetry collection is *Overwintering* (Oxford Poets/Carcanet, 2012).

SEAN O'BRIEN is Professor of Creative Writing at Newcastle University. His *Collected Poems* appeared from Picador in 2012 and his anthology, *Train Songs*, co-edited with Don Paterson, is forthcoming from Faber.